101
Science
Fair
Projects

by Kris Hirschmann

illustrated by Barbara Levy

To my husband, Mike,
for believing in me.
Thank you for helping me
turn my dreams into reality.

CONTENTS

Chapter 1

Science Fair or Science Fear?

The words "science fair" mean big science FEAR for many students. Are you one of them? Maybe you're nervous about your ability to complete such a big project. Maybe you're shy about putting your work on display. Maybe you don't like science very much. Or maybe you just have no idea where to start.

Why do so many kids groan when the words "science fair" are mentioned by their teachers? To answer this question, ask yourself what comes to mind when you think about science fair projects. Do you picture cool mechanical devices? ("Wow, I wouldn't have a clue how to make something like that!") In-depth explorations of topics you've never even heard of? ("How did they get that great idea?") Or how about fancy demonstrations using lots of expensive equipment? ("My parents would *never* buy me all that stuff.")

When you look at it that way, putting together a science fair project *can* seem pretty scary.

But here's the good news: Your project doesn't have to be

fancy, difficult, or expensive to be good. And most important, it doesn't have to be boring. A science fair project can be fascinating! Maybe you've always wondered why the sky is blue or how flies can walk upside down. Questions like these can be the perfect starting point for a blue-ribbon project. And picking something interesting or funny guarantees that you'll have a good time as you work.

This book includes 101 super science fair project ideas. Some are so easy that you can do them in an evening. Others will take several weeks and more research. No matter which idea you pick, chapters 2 through 5 will give you hints about how to put together a successful project, from start to finish.

Remember, the ideas in this book are just that: ideas. They're not step-by-step instructions. You will need to make your own decisions about how to conduct your experiments, record and display data, and set up controls. But enough information is included to give you a head start on each project. Don't be afraid to ask a parent or teacher for help if there is something you don't understand.

And don't forget the most important rule of all. *Make sure you are comfortable with the level of the project you choose.* "Wowing" the judges with equipment and big words is great, but if you don't fully understand your project, it will show. You'll learn more—and probably do better in the judging—if you pick a topic and a project you know you can handle and do a good, thorough job.

You see? It's not so scary after all. It's just a matter of knowing what to do—and you have this book to show you how. So turn the page. Let's change that science *fear* into science *flair*!

Science Fairs are Good for You!

You don't have to earn a ribbon to be a science fair winner. There are lots of reasons why participating in science fairs is good for you.

- One study showed that 67% of students who entered science fairs went on to earn four-year college degrees. That's more than double the national average! And a four-year degree means more exciting career options and higher earning potential down the road.

- The same study showed that science fair participants reported increased self confidence, self-image, thinking skills, goal-setting abilities, and respect from peers, whether or not they won any awards.

- By completing a science fair project, you'll become an expert on one little aspect of the scientific world. And it's just fun to know stuff!

Chapter 2

Planning a Path to Success

Would you travel to an unfamiliar place without looking at a map? Of course not. A map shows you where to go and gives you a way to check your progress during the journey.

You can look at your science fair project as a journey of discovery. And like any other journey, it needs a map. But you can't buy this map in a store. You have to create it yourself. A good *plan* is the map that will guide you as you work on your project. It will keep you on track and guarantee a safe arrival at your destination: science fair day!

There are four parts to the planning process: finding ideas, choosing a topic, outlining your procedure, and scheduling.

Finding Ideas

Some students worry more about finding a great idea than about any other part of a science fair project. But in reality, this is the easiest part. There are thousands of good ideas out there—far more than you have time to evaluate.

Here are some suggestions to help you start your search.

Read this book. Check out the 101 gooey, slimy, and tasty project ideas gathered here and see if anything catches your interest.

Visit the library. There are many books that list science fair project ideas. Some of these books are included in the bibliography on pages 92–94 at the back of this book. Your librarian will be able to recommend where to find these and other helpful sources.

Search the Internet. If you have computer access to the Internet, you can look for ideas online. Search under "Science Fair Projects." You will find dozens of web sites that can help you. Some good sites are listed in the bibliography at the back of this book.

Watch TV. You love to do this anyway, so why not make it part of your planning process? Science-minded kids' shows such as *Newton's Apple, Beakman's World,* and *Bill Nye the Science Guy* can give you good ideas. So can adult shows such as *National Geographic Explorer, The Crocodile Hunter,* and NOVA episodes.

Read the newspaper. Current events and issues such as hurricanes, wildfires, the ozone layer, oil spills, and pollution can inspire good science fair projects.

Look around. This may be the best way of all to get a project idea. What interests or puzzles you? Turn your burning questions into winning projects!

Choosing a Topic

There are so many fun project ideas that you might have trouble choosing just one. How can you decide?

The first and most important rule is this: *Choose a topic*

that interests you. Why be bored when you could be having fun? If you enjoy working on your project, you'll probably do a better job. You'll also gain knowledge that means something to you rather than ho-hum facts you don't care about.

Don't forget to consult the "local experts." It's likely that you have someone in your family who knows a lot about a science topic. For instance, if your mom is a dentist, you could do a project about teeth. A botany project might be perfect if your dad is a gardener. And your accountant aunt might not know much about science, but she will come in handy if you have a lot of numbers to graph. You need to do the work yourself, but it's always good to have people nearby who can help if you get stuck.

Finally, don't be afraid to be creative! An unusual topic is a good way for you to catch the judges' attention and earn a ribbon, as long as the project is well executed.

Fill out the Project Evaluation Form on page 15 to determine your project's potential. If your idea gets a good rating, you're in business! If it rates low on the scale, it could be a dud. You might want to keep looking.

Outlining Your Procedure

Once you have settled on a topic, think through your project and write down all the steps you must take.

Let's say you decide to do project #19 from this book, "Secret Fruit" (see page 39). Your list of tasks might look like this:

1. Do research to learn why lemon juice turns brown.
2. Do research about other fruits.
3. Based on research, form hypothesis about whether other fruit juices will do the same thing as lemon juice. (You will learn more about hypotheses in Chapter 3.)

4. Get fruit.
5. Conduct tests.
6. Write report.
7. Create science fair display.

Scheduling

Now look at your list and decide how long each step will take. The tasks above might break down like this: *Steps 1 through 3, one week. Step 4, one day. Step 5, two days. Step 6, one week. Step 7, two weeks.*

Adding it up gives you a total of four weeks and three days. So you should start your project at least that long before the science fair.

Always give yourself plenty of time when you make your schedule. For instance, if you think the research stage will take you two and a half hours, give yourself a week to get it done. Five half-hour sessions are easier than a single one-day marathon. And if things take a little longer than you expected, you'll have time to catch up.

Now that you've created your project plan, you're ready to do the work. On your mark . . . Get set . . . Go to page 17!

Boys vs. Girls

A 1991 study found that more males than females participate in science fairs. Males were more likely to choose topics in the physical sciences (chemistry, physics, mechanics). Females more often turned to biology for their ideas.

PROJECT EVALUATION FORM

Rank your proposed topic on each scale below. Add up the numbers, then read the rating chart at the bottom of the page to see how your project idea measures up.

Interest Level
1. Boring
2. OK, I guess
3. Interesting
4. Fascinating

Difficulty Level
1. Too hard
2. Too easy
3. Just right
4. It's a stretch, but I think I can handle it

Time Needed
1. Months of hard work
2. Just a few hours
3. A couple of days
4. A couple of weeks

Ease of Explanation
1. Very difficult to explain
2. Super simple
3. Can be explained well, but I need the proper research to back it up

Attractiveness
1. My display won't look good
2. I think it could look cool
3. I have a few good ideas already
4. The display I have in mind is awesome!

If you scored:

15 to 19 You've got a winning project!

12 to 14 Pretty good, but you might want to polish a few areas to make it really exceptional.

9 to 11 Borderline. This project could use some work.

8 or less Choose another project. This one has too many strikes against it.

Chapter 3

Acting Like a Scientist

Now that you have your science fair project planned out, it's time for the fun part: doing the work.

It can be tempting to leap right in and start exploring. But hold off for a moment. Do you think real scientists go into the lab and start throwing test tubes and chemicals around on a whim? Of course they don't. Scientists know exactly what they're trying to find out, and every step they take serves a purpose. You must do the same if you want your science fair project to succeed.

Using a procedure called the *scientific method* will help you to keep your project on track. There are five stages to the scientific method: purpose, hypothesis, procedure, results, and conclusion.

1. Purpose

Knowing your project's purpose simply means deciding what you're trying to find out. This is the part where you get specific.

As an example, let's say you are fascinated by butterflies.

You decide to make them your science fair topic. But "butterflies" isn't very specific. You need a direction—something to figure out. After thinking about butterflies and the many interesting things they do, you decide to find out if you can predict the type of butterfly a caterpillar will turn into. That's a good purpose because it's a question with a solid answer.

2. Hypothesis

Once you have determined the purpose of the experiment, you must state what you think will happen. This statement is called the *hypothesis*. Through your experiments, the hypothesis will either be accepted (you were right) or rejected (you were wrong).

When forming your hypothesis, don't just make a guess. Do some research to learn a little bit about your topic.

Let's go back to the butterfly example. Before forming your hypothesis, you could go to the library and look for books on caterpillars and butterflies. You discover that many fine nature guides show full-color pictures of caterpillars and the butterflies they turn into. Based on this information, you might hypothesize that your predictions will be successful.

3. Procedure

Finally, you get to do the experiment! In our butterfly project, that means capturing caterpillars and setting up a comfortable home with plenty of food for each one. The next step would be identifying each caterpillar using the nature guides you found while researching your hypothesis. In the final step, you would watch over time as each caterpillar spun a cocoon and eventually emerged as a butterfly.

Our example is easy. But other experiments may not be

so simple to figure out. If you're not sure about the best way to conduct your experiment, ask a teacher for help.

Don't forget to record everything you do while conducting your experiments. You will need the information when the time comes to write your . . .

4. Results

What did you find out? Did you accept or reject your hypothesis? Use charts, graphs, and pictures to demonstrate your findings. Present solid numbers and facts, not opinions.

5. Conclusion

Now is the time to present your opinion. What did you learn while doing your project?

Maybe everything went as planned and you accepted your hypothesis. Congratulations! But even if your hypothesis was wrong, you still learned something. Let's take one final look at the butterfly project:

"I predicted some of the butterflies correctly, but some were wrong. I learned that many caterpillars look alike. When identifying caterpillars, it is important to look very carefully for small markings and read the book to see if the markings are mentioned. If I did this experiment again, I think I would do it better because I would be more careful."

At the science fair, the judges won't care that this student's hypothesis was wrong. But they *will* care that he or she understood what happened.

You've planned and you've experimented. That's two big chunks of work done. Now it's time for the final push: creating your display.

Chapter 4

Sometimes You're Allowed to Show Off

You are finally ready to produce your science fair display—the summary of everything you have done so far.

You might think your display is only one small part of your project. After all, you may have done weeks of work before getting to this point. But your display is the *only* part most people will see. This is your one opportunity to tell the world how much work you did and how many cool things you learned. If you don't do a good job, they won't be able to appreciate your efforts.

So be a showoff. A science fair is one time when showing off is okay—especially if you want to win a ribbon!

The Basics

Before you begin, check to see if there are any size or format requirements for your display. Many science fairs require participants to use a three-panel display board of a set size. Even if your school doesn't require this setup, consider using it anyway. It's a time-honored way to get your information across.

Your display should include a brief summary of your project (including your hypothesis), a write-up of your procedure, graphs or tables showing your data, and a conclusion.

Standing Out from the Crowd

Your display has to be eye-catching as well as informative. What good is a brilliant report if no one looks at it?

What's in a Name?

The first step to an attention-grabbing science fair display is a catchy title. Consider the following titles:

Which Grows Faster, Human Hair or Animal Fur?
or
MAN VS. MUTT!

Both titles refer to project #29 in this book. Which one do you think would catch *your* eye across a room? If you're like most people, you'll find the shorter, funkier title more appealing—especially if it appears in big, bold letters at the top of the project.

Don't forget that people need to understand your title. If your snappy title doesn't really tell what the project is, include a subtitle that explains things more clearly. Combine the two titles above:

MAN VS. MUTT!
Which Grows Faster, Human Hair or Animal Fur?

to grab attention and explain the project, too.

Colors, Photos, and Displays

You've made your project sound good. Now you need to make it look good.

Your goal is to create a display that is colorful but not jumbled. Pick no more than two or three main colors for your lettering and background. And choose your colors well. Whoever heard of a blue volcano? Your colors should match your subject (for instance, fiery reds, oranges, and yellows for volcanoes; leafy greens and earthy browns for plants).

Photos, graphs, and displays of equipment or materials add the finishing touches. Use them well to create a truly memorable science fair project.

* * *

The last line has been drawn and the last picture is pasted. Whew! You're finished . . . or are you? Not quite. You still have one more hurdle to leap: the judging. But don't worry. If you've done your work up to this point, you should be nearly ready. Turn to Chapter 5 to learn what the judges are looking for and what you can do to prepare.

Chapter 5

Getting a Jump
on the Judges

Throughout your project, you have made decisions. You decided on a topic; you decided on a hypothesis and a procedure; and you decided how to display your work. The only person you had to please was yourself.

But get ready. It all changes on science fair day. That's when the *(eek!)* JUDGES come around and tell you what *they* think of your work. They might even want to talk to you about your project!

Being judged is always scary, but you can make it a little less frightening by being prepared. And you can get prepared by knowing what the judges are looking for. Science fair judging can be broken down into six categories: creativity, scientific thought, thoroughness, skill, comprehension, and neatness.

Creativity

Did you come up with an unusual topic? Did you find a creative way to explore an old topic? Did you design any of the equipment used in your project? Judges reward these and other types of creativity with extra points.

Scientific Thought

In this category, judges will evaluate your methods. Was your procedure effective? Did you draw good conclusions based on the evidence?

Thoroughness

Did you explore your topic thoroughly? Did you do only one experiment or did you repeat it at least once to be sure of your results? How good are your notes? These are the types of things the judges will look for in this category.

Skill

Judges don't just want to see that you did something. They want to see that you did it well. Does your project demonstrate technical skill? Did you do everything by yourself, or did you get a lot of help? A skillful scientist will earn better ratings.

Comprehension

This category is very important. It may also be the scariest. Why? Because the judges might want to interview you to see how well you understand your subject. To prepare, make a list of important concepts you should know. Let friends or family quiz you on this material in the days before the fair. You should also review your notes just before the judging. If you've done your work properly, your understanding should shine through without any trouble.

Neatness

Neatness counts. Your project should look tidy, and so

should you. Dress well and wow the judges with your sense of style.

You've read it all, from getting an idea to surviving the judging. Now it's time to do it! The rest of this book is filled with great science fair project ideas. You can follow these ideas exactly or apply your own personal twist. Use the titles provided or make up your own. Most important, have fun. Remember that science fear? Forget about it. This is where you turn into a science fair *superstar*!

An Example of Wrong Thinking

The famous scientist was doing a demonstration before a crowd. He set two frogs on a table. One was a fine specimen, big and strong. The other, sadly, had been born with no legs.

The scientist leaned down and looked the four-legged frog in the eye. "Jump, froggy!" he exclaimed. The frog immediately leaped high into the air.

The scientist next approached the legless frog. He leaned down. He eyed the frog. Then . . . "Jump, froggy!" But the frog did nothing.

The scientist frowned. "Jump, froggy!" he said again, a little louder this time. But the frog still didn't move.

Finally the scientist turned to face the crowd. "You see?" he said grandly. "When the frog's legs are removed, it loses its hearing."

The scientist in this story used poor reasoning. Don't let it happen to you! Think carefully about your conclusions. The judges will notice any gaps in your scientific thinking.

Chapter 6

Play With Your Food

1. Sweet Surprise: Do Candies Vary in Density?

Category: Chemistry

Density is how much weight a material crams into a certain amount of space. Do different types of candy have different densities? Try this project to find out. Gather all of your favorite types of candy and remove the packaging. Find the mass (weight) of each candy using a scientific scale (ask your teacher if your school has one of these special scales). Then find the volume of each candy by submerging it in a graduated cylinder full of water. Divide the mass by the volume to get the density (Density = Mass÷Volume). Which candy is the most dense? Which is the least dense?

2. The Crunch Challenge: Which Cereal Stays Crispy Longest?

Category: Chemistry

Soggy cereal stinks! But you can avoid this breakfast bummer. Test several cereals to see which one keeps its crunch the longest after you add milk. If the cereals behave differently, try to figure out why (for example, do sugar-coated cereals stay crunchy longer than Cheerios?). HINT: Most grocery stores sell variety packs that contain single servings of several different cereals. You could also ask friends to bring you a handful of their favorite cereal in a plastic zipper bag.

3. Counting Calories: Are Heavier Foods More Fattening?

Category: Chemistry/Physics

Calories measure how much energy a food puts into your body. High-calorie foods give us lots of energy. But if you don't burn all the calories, they get stored as fat. Do you think heavier foods have more calories? Weigh different foods (fruits and veggies, candy, oils, pasta, rice, meat, soda, juice, etc.), then look up the number of calories in each food. (Packaged foods have calories listed on their labels. To find the calories in fruits, veggies, and other unpackaged foods, you will need a reference from your local library. Ask the librarian for help.) What do you discover? Are heavier foods more likely to make you fat?

4. I Got the Blues: The Probability of Choosing a Blue M&M

Category: Mathematics

Put a bunch of M&Ms into a container. Without looking, reach in and pull out one M&M at a time. Record the color of each candy you remove. How many blue M&Ms do you think you will choose if you pull out 100 candies? HINT: Think about how you want to approach this project. You could just dump a big bag of M&Ms into the container and get started. You could count out equal amounts of the different colors first. You could even do the experiment both ways and compare your results. It would take longer, but it would be more scientific. Ask a few friends to help you do your experiment to make it more fun.

5. Colorful Cubes: Which Ice Cube Melts the Fastest?
Category: Physics

Will ice cubes of different colors melt at different speeds? Use food coloring to make a tray full of ice cubes in all the colors of the rainbow. Then set the colorful cubes in the sun. Use a stopwatch to get an accurate melting time for each cube. Do some colors melt faster than others? Try it a couple of times to see if your results are consistent. You could also try melting another set of cubes in the shade instead of the sun to see if there is any difference.

6. Water Weight: How Much Water Is In a Bunch of Grapes?
Category: Chemistry

Did you know that raisins are just grapes in disguise? It's true! Raisins are made by removing most of the moisture from grapes. You can easily find out how much water is in a bunch of grapes. Weigh a handful of grapes (remove them from the stem first). Then set them in a warm place or in the oven (get an adult's help) to dry. Once all the grapes have shriveled into raisins, weigh them again. The weight difference shows you how much water has evaporated.

7. Freaky Food: Strange Behavior in the Microwave

Category: Physics

Microwave ovens have an unusual effect on some foods. Two you might be familiar with are popcorn, which explodes, and bread, which gets mushy. Can you find other foods that behave strangely in the microwave? (Here are some ideas to get you started: marshmallows, grapes, hot dogs, soda.) Put a sample of each food into its own plastic zipper bag or in a plastic container to prevent messes. Then ask an adult helper to cook each food for a minute in the microwave. Watch through the window and record anything unusual you see. Can you explain the effects you notice?

NOTE: Be careful when removing hot foods from the microwave.

8. A Fat-Finding Mission: Identifying High-Fat Foods by Their Stains

Category: Chemistry

Some foods leave greasy stains. Do you think the size of the stain has anything to do with the fattiness of the food? Test it out by putting different foods on pieces of brown paper. (Grocery bags are perfect.) Label the samples and let them sit for fifteen minutes. Then remove the food and let the pieces of paper dry for a day. Check for stains. Do the fattiest foods leave the biggest stains? (Packaged foods have the total percentage of fat listed on their labels. To find the fat percentage of unpackaged foods, you will need a reference from your local library. Ask the librarian for help.)

9. Spore Portraits: Making Mushroom Art

Category: Microbiology

Mushrooms constantly drop *spores* (seeds) into the air. On its own, a spore is too small to see. But when many spores pile up in the same place, they become visible. How can you prove this is true? Try making spore prints. Cut off the cap of a mushroom (the upper bulging part) and set it gill-side down on a piece of white paper. Let it sit overnight. When you lift the cap, you'll find a delicate ribbed print underneath. Try as many types of mushrooms as possible to get prints of different colors and shapes!

10. Fizz or Fizzle: Does Soda Lose Its Fizz Faster When It's Cold or Warm?

Category: Chemistry

We all know that soda loses its fizz, or bubbles, after a while. That's because soda contains a gas called *carbon dioxide* that slowly escapes into the air. When all the gas is gone, so are the bubbles. Does temperature make a difference? Find out! Pour equal amounts of soda into three identical clear cups. Then put one in the refrigerator, one on the counter, and one in the sun. Record each soda's temperature and fizz factor (the amount of bubbles in the soda) after fifteen minutes. Continue to record your data at fifteen-minute intervals for the next hour. Which soda is the first to go flat? Which stays fizzy the longest?

11. Go with the Flow: Does Cooling Increase Viscosity?
Category: Physics

A liquid's flow speed is referred to as its *viscosity*. Thick liquids (such as honey) have a high viscosity; thin ones (such as water) have a low viscosity. Do you think you can make a liquid's viscosity higher by cooling it? Test it. You could try water, oil, syrup, honey, shampoo, or anything else you like. Put a spoonful of each liquid at the top of a slope (a cookie sheet with a raised end is perfect). Time how long it takes each liquid to reach the bottom of the slope. Then put all the liquids in the refrigerator for a few hours, and repeat the process. (Be sure not to let the liquids get mixed up.) Do the liquids take longer to reach the bottom of the slope when they are cold?

12. A Rotten Project: Does a Fruit's Skin Protect It from Germs?
Category: Microbiology

Your skin prevents germs from getting into your body. Do you think a fruit's skin serves the same purpose? To find out, buy a few apples. Scrape some of them hard enough to break the skin in several places. Then introduce bacteria by licking the scrapes. You could spray or rub an infection-preventing medicine such as Neosporin or Bacitracin onto a few (but not all) of the apples. Do the scraped apples rot more quickly than the ones you didn't scrape? Did the medicine seem to help stop the rotting process? What conclusions can you draw about the function of a fruit's skin?

13. Pop Quiz: The Density of Regular vs. Diet Soda

Category: Chemistry

Regular soda is full of sugar. Diet soda has no sugar, just sweetening chemicals. Will all the sugar in regular soda increase its density (see #1 for a definition)? A bucket of water will let you put it to the test. Get several cans of regular soda flavors and their diet versions. Put them in the water one by one and see how quickly they sink to the bottom. (Some might even float!) The fastest sinkers are the most dense; the slowest sinkers (or highest floaters) are the least dense.

14. Gelatin Lenses: Exploring Optics with Jell-O®

Category: Physics

Concave lenses (edges thicker than the middle) make things look smaller. *Convex* lenses (edges thinner than the middle) make things look larger. Do you think the lens material (usually glass or plastic) causes this effect, or is it the shape of the lens? Find out by making and testing gelatin lenses. To mold the gelatin into the correct shapes, you'll need some special materials: two watch glasses (curved pieces of glass) and two petri dishes. Ask your teacher to help you locate these materials. You could also order them from Science Stuff, a science supply store, at 1-800-795-7315, or online at http://sciencestuff.com/products.htm. Once the lenses are made, set them on a newspaper, a book, or a magazine and look through them. What happens to the type and pictures beneath the lenses?

Chapter 7

Sticky, Slimy, Gross, and Weird

15. The Tooth Truth: Which Liquid Is Most Harmful to Teeth?

Category: Chemistry

"That stuff will rot your teeth!" You've probably heard your parents or your dentist say that a hundred times. But is it true? Find out for yourself. Get six or seven teeth from a dentist. Place each tooth in a different type of liquid. Try regular soda, diet soda, orange juice, vinegar, water, sports drink, coffee, milk, iced tea, or anything else people often drink. Check the teeth every day and record any changes you notice. Do you see any decay? Which liquid is really the worst for your teeth?

16. Bad to the Bone: Which Liquid Is Most Harmful to Bones?

Category: Chemistry

This project is similar to #15. But bones and teeth are made of different materials, so your results will be different. Some liquids remove the hard minerals from bones. The bones look normal, but they feel strangely rubbery! How long will it take for different liquids to turn bones into "rubber"? To find out, save and clean a bunch of chicken bones of similar size (the bones from chicken wings are ideal). Submerge each bone in a different type of liquid (try vinegar, lemon juice, cola, orange juice, water, or anything else you like). Check the bones every day and record any changes you notice.

17. Stick 'em Up: Which Homemade Glue Works Best?

Category: Chemistry

These days, big companies make glue and sell it in stores. But in the past, people made their own glue from materials found around the home. A few common materials that can be used as glue are *casein* (a thick protein found in milk); flour-and-water paste; and cornstarch. With a little research, you can find out how to make these and other types of homemade glues. Once you've made a variety, test them all to see which one works best.

18. Slime Coat: Does Slug Slime Work as a Sealant?

Category: Chemistry

A *sealant* fills or coats cracks and joints. A traveling slug uses its slime for exactly this purpose. The slime smooths bumps and cracks, thus protecting the slug's squishy body. Is slug slime strong enough to seal cracks? Find out by poking a few small holes in three Ping-Pong balls. Use a cotton swab to CAREFULLY take some slime from a slug. Cover the balls' holes with slime and allow several hours of drying time. Then submerge one ball in a sink, leave one out in the rain, and put one in the dishwasher. (Turn a glass or cup upside-down over the ball to keep it from bouncing around too much.) Does any water get into the balls? If not, your sealant did its job!

19.Secret Fruit: Which Juices Act as Invisible Ink?

Category: Chemistry

Making invisible ink from lemons is a classic experiment. You simply wet a cotton swab with lemon juice and use it to write a message on a piece of white paper. Allow the juice to dry. The message is invisible . . . until it's heated, that is. A few minutes over a lightbulb or toaster causes a chemical change in the lemon juice. It turns brown, and your message becomes visible. Do you think you can achieve the same results using other juices? Compare lemon juice to orange, apple, cranberry, grapefruit, and any other juices you like.

20.Bearded Bread: Which Type of Bread Molds the Fastest?

Category: Microbiology

You're never safe from mold spores. They're everywhere—even in the bread you eat. Prove it with this project. Get as many different types of bread as you can (white, wheat, rye, sourdough, with or without preservatives, etc.). Gather one piece of each type. Let all the pieces sit outdoors in the open air for five to ten minutes. Then put each piece into a plastic zipper bag and label each bag. Set all the bags in a warm place and check them every day. Which bread molds first? How many different types of mold can you see among all the bags? Ask a librarian to help you find sources that give examples of various types of mold.

21. Household Mold: Which Parts of My Home Hide Spores?

Category: Microbiology

Any dusty place is a haven for mold spores. Are there spores hiding in your home? This project is very similar to #20. But instead of using different types of bread, use several slices from the same loaf. Rub each slice along a different surface in your home. You can try any areas you like, but here are some suggestions: a windowsill, a bathtub, a countertop, an air conditioner filter, a carpet, a TV screen. Put each slice into a plastic zipper bag and label each bag. Then sit back and watch your mold garden grow. Which area of your home sprouts mold the quickest?

22. Yeast Feast: Does Yeast Grow Best in Warm, Cold, or Hot Water?

Category: Microbiology

Unlike most food products, yeast is alive! These tiny one-celled fungi come alive and start growing when combined with water and sugar. Do you think yeast will grow best under warm, cold, or hot conditions? Put $\frac{1}{2}$ tablespoon (7.4 ml) each of yeast and sugar into three identical containers. To one container, add a tablespoon (14.8 ml) of cold water. To another, add a tablespoon (14.8 ml) of warm water. To the last, add a tablespoon (14.8 ml) of hot water. Shake or stir each container, then watch as the yeast feasts. Which temperature seems best for yeast growth?

23. Soil and Spoil: Do Foods Decompose Faster When Buried?

Category: Microbiology

If you don't eat them, foods eventually *decompose* (break

down into their simpler components). Bacteria and fungi are responsible for this process. Most of these micro-organisms live in soil. So do you think foods decay faster when buried? Get two cucumbers of about the same size. Leave one sitting on your counter. Bury the other. (Mark the spot with a stake so you can find it easily.) Dig up the buried cucumber once a day to check its progress. Which cucumber rots fastest? HINT: You could expand this project by testing many different types of food.

24. Balloon Bloat: Which Decaying Food Makes the Most Gas?

Category: Microbiology

As foods decay, they create gas. Do all decaying foods give off the same amount of gas? To discover the answer, get a few empty, dry 2-liter soda bottles and some balloons. Weigh out equal amounts of different fruits and veggies. Put one type of food into each bottle. (It's okay if you have to chop it up.) Throw a spoonful

(any size spoon will do) of dirt into each bottle to add bacteria, then seal each bottle with a balloon. As the foods decay, they will release enough gas to inflate the balloons a little bit. Measure the balloons every day to see which bottle contains the most gas.

25. Body Dandruff: Does All Human Skin Flake at the Same Rate?

Category: Physiology

Your skin takes a lot of abuse. It gets rubbed, bumped, scratched, and scraped all day, every day. As a result, the *epidermis* (the outer layer of your skin) is constantly flaking off. Do all parts of your skin flake at the same rate, or do some areas wear off more quickly? Find out by staining different areas of your skin with a permanent marker. Go nuts! Mark high-abuse areas such as the soles of your feet and your elbows. Also mark low-abuse areas such as your belly button and your earlobes. Try to guess the order in which the marks will disappear. How good are your predictions? NOTE: ASK A PARENT FOR PERMISSION BEFORE BEGINNING THIS EXPERIMENT.

26. It's Raining Rocks: Collecting Micrometeorites from Rainwater

Category: Astronomy

Millions of tiny meteors bombard us every day. When they reach the earth's surface, these itsy-bitsy space rocks are called *micrometeorites*. You can collect and examine these rocks. Put a container outdoors the next time it rains. After the rain stops, bring the container inside and let all the water evaporate. Small particles will remain. Brush them onto a plastic sheet and hold a magnet underneath the sheet. Shake the sheet to get rid of non-magnetic particles. Those that remain are likely to be micrometeorites! Examine your space rocks with a strong magnifying glass or a microscope. Discuss what you see.

27. Rubber Eggs: The Effect of Shell Color on Dissolving Speed

Category: Chemistry

The "Rubber Egg" is a popular—and spectacular—experiment. A hard-boiled egg is submerged in vinegar and left to sit for several days. The vinegar slowly dissolves the eggshell. But even after the eggshell is gone, the egg holds its shape due to a tough membrane that surrounds the insides. Impress the judges with a display of these yucky, rubbery eggs. Make it a good science fair project by testing to see if eggshells of different colors (white, brown, speckled) react differently to the vinegar. You can also make your eggs every color of the rainbow with an egg-dyeing kit. Check frequently to see which egg turns to "rubber" the fastest.

28. Fast Fingers, Twinkle Toes: Growth Rates of Fingernails vs. Toenails

Category: Physiology

Which do you think grow faster, your fingernails or your toenails? Find out with this simple project. Cut all your nails as short as you can. Measure each nail and record its length. Check and measure each nail once a week up until the science fair. What do you learn? HINT: To achieve the best results, you'll need to start this project early. Try to give yourself six full weeks of growing time. And it goes without saying that you shouldn't cut—or bite!—any of your nails during this time.

Chapter 8

Animals as Science Pals

29. Man vs. Mutt: Which Grows Faster, Human Hair or Animal Fur?

Category: Physiology/Zoology

Get permission from a parent before doing this experiment. You're going to look funny for a while, and so is your pet. But the science learning makes it worthwhile! Ask a grown-up to shave areas of equal size on your head and your pet's back. Then monitor and record the hair growth in these areas over the next four to six weeks. Make sure you take lots of pictures if you want your display to be really spectacular. And remember, you don't have to limit yourself to one pet. If you have several furry friends who can participate, all the better.

30. Fishy Business: Does a Mirror Change My Fish's Behavior?

Category: Animal Behavior

Pet fish do the same things every day—a little swimming, a little eating, maybe even a little digging. Do you think your fish would do anything different if you held a mirror up to the tank? Spend some time watching your fish from a distance. Take notes on everything it does. Then approach the tank. See what the fish does when you stand nearby. Finally, hold a mirror close enough to the tank for the fish to get a good look. (Make sure sunlight isn't reflecting off the mirror into the tank.) What does the fish do now? For the most scientific results, repeat this experiment several times.

31. Get a Whiff of This: Exploring Worms' Sense of Smell

Category: Zoology

Do you think worms have a sense of smell? If so, what smells do they like and dislike? You can't ask the worms, but you can expose them to different smells and see how they behave. Dig up a few worms or buy some from your local bait shop. Gather some materials with strong smells (try vanilla extract, syrup, potpourri, perfume, or anything else you like). Put some of each substance near each worm's head (make sure your samples are separated so each worm is reacting only to the scent near its head). See whether the worms approach the substance or turn away. Do all the worms like the same smells? If so, why do you think this is true?

32. Cocoon Surprise: Predicting Butterflies from Caterpillars

Category: Zoology

Capture several types of caterpillars. Set each one up in its own special home (check your library to find out how to properly care for caterpillars). Then try to predict what type of butterfly or moth each caterpillar will turn into. To do this, consult an insect identification book. When you think you have identified all the caterpillars, sit back and wait. After a while the caterpillars will spin cocoons and begin the transformation process. When they emerge as butterflies and moths, go back to the insect books. Were your predictions right? HINT: Start this experiment as early as possible. You can't rush Mother Nature.

33. Microbe Mouth: Does Human or Dog Saliva Contain More Bacteria?

Category: Microbiology

It's not pleasant to think about, but here's the fact: Human spit is full of bacteria. But what about your dog? Is its mouth cleaner or dirtier than yours? Find out by taking spit samples from yourself and your dog. Spread the samples onto sterile agar plates and wait a few days for bacteria colonies to grow. (You can probably get agar plates from your science teacher. You could also contact Science Stuff, a science supply store, at 1-800-795-7315, or online at http://sciencestuff.com/products.htm.) Don't be afraid to ask for help. Bacteria grows best in special conditions that your science teacher can explain to you. Which samples grow the most bacteria, yours or your dog's? Repeat the experiment, but this time brush your teeth and tongue before you take your saliva sample. Did the results change?

34. Ants Marching: What Happens If You Break the Trail?

Category: Animal Behavior

You have probably seen an ant trail—a line of many ants marching one behind the other. Although the ants seem to know where they're going, they really don't. They are following a chemical trail laid down by earlier ants. If you break the trail, will the ants be able to find their way back to it? Interrupt the trail using larger and larger objects. (For instance, you could start by laying a pin across the trail, then a pencil, then a thick marker, etc.) Can the ants stick to the trail with an object in the way? Does the size of the object make a difference? Answer these and any other questions that occur to you.

35. Insect Appeal: What Color Lightbulb Attracts the Most Bugs?

Category: Animal Behavior

When the porch lights go on at night, the insects start to swarm. The instinct to move toward light is called *phototaxis,* and bugs are famous for it. Do you think the color of a light affects its insect appeal? Get several colored lightbulbs (available at most hardware stores). You could try white, yellow, blue, red, green, and even black light. Ask an adult to screw a bulb into an outdoor socket. Hang strips of flypaper near the light and wait until the sun goes down. Turn the light on for a measured period of time, then count how many bugs you captured. Repeat with each lightbulb. Rate the bulbs according to their critter-catching power.

36. Chirpometer: Does Cricket Chirp Rate Reflect Temperature?

Category: Zoology

You may have heard that you can tell the temperature by counting a cricket's chirps. Is that really true, or is it just an old wives' tale? Do this project to find out. Here's the formula: Number of chirps in 14 seconds + 40 = Temperature in degrees Fahrenheit. Now get outside with your thermometer and your stopwatch and find some crickets! Take readings at different times of the day so you can get a wide range of temperature conditions. And use a few different crickets, too. Some may be more accurate than others.

37. What's Up, Doc: Do Rabbits Really Love Carrots?

Category: Animal Behavior

Everyone knows that rabbits love carrots. Or do they? Maybe it's just a rumor started by Bugs Bunny. Test to see if carrots really are your pet rabbit's favorite snack. Set out small amounts of several foods (you could try cabbage, lettuce, fruit, nuts, and dry pellets in addition to carrots). Record which one your rabbit eats first. Do this every day for at least a week. Use the same foods each time, but change the arrangement of the food (for example, if you put carrots in the center of the group the first time, move them to the end the next time). What does your pet really think of carrots?

38. Crazy Kitties: Does Catnip Have the Same Effect on All Cats?

Category: Animal Behavior

The herb *catnip* is often used in cat toys. It has a reputation for making kitties behave strangely. Typical behaviors include pawing, kicking, and rolling. Does catnip have the same effect on every cat? Ask as many cat owners as possible to volunteer their pets for your project. (NEVER feed anything to an animal without the owner's permission.) Get some dried catnip from a pet store and give a measured amount to each cat. Then observe and record each cat's response. Do they all do the same things? Are there some cats who don't seem to respond at all? Do younger cats and kittens react differently than older cats?

39. Tickle Me Fido: Testing My Dog's Scratch Response

Category: Animal Behavior

Sometimes when you scratch a dog behind the ear or on the belly the dog's back leg starts kicking. This is the "scratch" or "tickle" response, and most dogs have it. Test your dog's scratch response. Is it specific to one area, or can you activate it by scratching in several places? Does it have to be a scratch or will a tickle work? If you scratch faster, will the dog kick faster? Research why some dogs respond this way when tickled or scratched on certain parts of their bodies. One good thing: Your dog will enjoy this project as much as you do!

40. Ding Dong! Training My Pet to Come When the Doorbell Rings

Category: Animal Behavior

Animals can be trained to do many wonderful tricks. The easiest way is to provide a reward, such as food, when the animal does what you want it to do. See this theory in action by training your pet (dogs or cats respond well to training) to come at the sound of the doorbell. Get a bunch of small tasty treats and stand by the door with your pet. Have a friend ring the doorbell. Immediately give your pet a treat. Repeat this process several times. Then let your pet wander away to where it can't see you. Have your friend ring the doorbell again. If your pet doesn't come on its own, call it to you and give it a treat. Repeat the process as often as necessary (don't get discouraged if it takes a few weeks). After a while your pet will realize that the sound of the doorbell means food. Watch it come running when it hears the ring!

☆ DO SPORTS DRINKS ☆ IMPROVE PERFORMANCE?

Activity	Gatorade	Water	Powerade
high jump	2'1"	2'3"	2'
50-yard dash	35 sec.	35 sec.	33 sec.
run around block	2 min.	2 min.	2 min.
50 jumping jacks	45 sec.	50 sec.	48 sec.
25 sit-ups	1 min.	59 sec.	1 min., 2 sec.
goal kicks	12 of 20	10 of 20	8 of 20
long jump	4'	3'9"	3'6"
10 free throws	6 of 10	8 of 10	7 of 10
swim 1 lap	25 sec.	22 sec.	23 sec.
run up 12 stairs	15 sec.	18 sec.	18 sec.

Chapter 9

The Commercial Challenge

41. Suck It Up: Which Paper Towel Holds the Most Liquid?

Category: Chemistry

Some manufacturers claim their paper towels pick up more liquid than others. Is it true? Collect as many different types of paper towel as you can (make sure the paper towel sheets are all about the same size). Crumple up one of the towels and set it in a strainer. Fill a measuring cup with one cup (240 ml) of water. Then pour water very slowly onto the towel. The towel is *saturated* (full of moisture) when water starts to drip through the strainer. Record how much water you used before the towel became saturated. Repeat with each paper towel. Which brand wins the water war? Do thicker paper towels really absorb more water?

42. Go For It: Do Sports Drinks Improve Performance?

Category: Physiology

Some ads suggest that sports drinks can make us leap higher, run faster, and play longer. Test the claims! Get a few athletic volunteers. Invent a "sports test" with a couple of categories. For instance, you could include leaping height and time to run around the block. Give your volunteers a drink of Gatorade, then tell them to wait twenty minutes. Have the volunteers complete the test. Record the results. Repeat the test one week later. But this time, use Powerade instead. The following week, try Allsport. The final week, use regular water. Does the type of drink seem to make a difference? If so, why do you think some drinks helped the volunteers to perform better? Do you think other factors may have been involved (for example, the volunteers were not well rested or the weather was hot)?

43. Sweat Busters: Which Works Better, Antiperspirant or Deodorant?

Category: Chemistry/Physiology

We use both antiperspirants and deodorants to get rid of stinky body odor. But the two products are supposed to work in different ways. Deodorants stop your sweat from stinking; antiperspirants stop you from sweating. Are these claims true? Get as many different types of antiperspirants and deodorants as you can. Smear a brand in your armpits. Exercise until you break a sweat. Then press a paper towel against each armpit. Measure the moisture marks to rate the "dampness factor." Repeat with each brand, washing with soap and water between each trial. Do you sweat less when using antiperspirants? Do some products work better than others?

44. Fat Full or Fat Free: Can You Taste the Difference?
Category: Physiology

Some food manufacturers make fat-free versions of their regular food. (You can buy fat-free potato chips, hot dogs, cheese, and buttery-tasting spreads, to name just a few.) These companies say you can't tell the difference. Will this statement pass the test? You'll need several volunteers to find out. Get the regular and fat-free versions of a few different foods. Blindfold all your volunteers, then give them food samples. Repeat the experiment several times to ensure accuracy. Ask them to identify the fat-free versions. What results do you get?

45. The Pepsi Challenge: Results of a Blind Taste Test
Category: Physiology

In The Pepsi Challenge, people taste two unidentified soft drinks. One is Coca-Cola; one is Pepsi. This commercial implies that Pepsi is so good, even Coke drinkers will say it tastes better. Is this claim true? Ask your school for permission to set up The Pepsi Challenge during a busy time, such as a sporting event. Put up a sign to attract volunteers. Ask each volunteer whether he or she prefers Coke or Pepsi. Then provide a sample of each drink in an unmarked cup. Ask the volunteer to pick the better-tasting drink. Does Pepsi really win, or do most people pick the soda they named? Why do you think some people can taste a difference between the two types of soda?

46. The Great Pop-Off: Which Brand of Microwave Popcorn Is Best?

Category: Physics

Every popcorn maker declares that their brand is the best. But which one wins the blue ribbon in real life? You can test for a couple of things. First, see which brand pops best. Second, see which brand pops biggest. Answer these questions by counting out 100 unpopped kernels of each brand you wish to test. Microwave each batch according to each brand's cooking instructions. Count to see how many unpopped kernels are left in each batch. Then measure the volume of each by putting it into a measuring cup. Most popped kernels + Most volume = The winner!

47. The Big Blow-Off: Which Brand of Bubble Gum Makes the Biggest Bubbles?

Category: Chemistry

Do you think some types of gum let you blow bigger bubbles than others? Find out by gathering several types of bubble gum. Weigh out an equal amount of each. Test one of the gums by chewing until it's soft, then blow several bubbles as big as you can. Measure and record the size of each bubble. (Ask a friend to do the measuring.) Find the average size of the bubbles you blew. Repeat with the other gums. Is there a difference in bubble size?

48. Shower Power: Which Mold Killer Works Best?

Category: Chemistry/Microbiology

There are lots of products on the market that claim to make household mold disappear. Which one works best? Get a few brands of mold- and mildew-killing cleaners (Tilex, Tile Plus, X-14, etc.). Then find a spot that could use a little cleanup. (The "mold monster" often hides in the folds of your shower curtain.) Squirt each type of cleaner in a different area and time how long it takes the mold to disappear. Which cleaner works best? WARNING: Ask an adult for help with this project. Household cleaners can be dangerous when sprayed in an enclosed area.

49. Going and Going . . . Which Battery Lasts Longest?

Category: Physics

You know the Energizer bunny. He keeps going and going and going . . . But do Energizer batteries really last longer than other brands? It's not hard to find out. Get a battery-operated object that you can leave on for hours at a time. (A flashlight is perfect.) Insert new Energizer batteries and turn the object on. Leave it on until the batteries fail. Record the time. Then insert new batteries of a different brand and repeat. Try this experiment with as many brands as possible (use both the big names and the store brands). How does the bunny's brand stack up?

50. Stuck On You: Which Bandage Sticks Best?

Category: Chemistry

It seems like every brand of adhesive bandage (Band-Aid, Curad, etc.) claims to stick best in the water. Which one really gets the job done? Get as many brands of bandages as you can. (Make sure they're all about the same size.) Stick one bandage of each brand to your leg. Then fill your bathtub with water and sit in it for five minutes. Make sure the bandages stay underwater. Do some of them come off? Do some stick longer than others? Repeat the experiment by placing bandages on your arms, feet, and hands. Which brand of bandage do you think is best?

51. Its Lips Are Sealed: Which Type of Plastic Zipper Bag Is Best?

Category: Physics

Hefty, Ziploc, and Gladlock are a few types of zipper bags. There are also a lot of no-name brands. Are some better than others? Gather a few samples of each and find out. Put an equal amount of water into each bag. Try a shake test (shake hard for a couple of minutes) and a pressure test (put weight on the bag). Do any of the bags leak? You could also put the bags into the freezer to see how they perform. You could even squirt a little perfume or cologne into each bag, then check for escaping scents. Which bag will keep your lunch safe?

52. Pearly Whites: Does Whitening Toothpaste Work?

Category: Chemistry

Certain toothpastes are advertised as whitening agents. Over time, they are supposed to brighten your teeth. Pick a brand . . . any brand . . . and find out if it's true! Take a picture of your teeth before you begin. Then brush your teeth as normal, with one little difference. Use regular toothpaste on your top teeth, but use the whitening paste on the bottom. Take a picture of your teeth once a week for at least a month. Does the whitening paste do its job? HINT: Don't worry about having different colors of teeth. If the whitening paste works, you can fix your top teeth after the science fair is over.

53. Foam Facts: Do Some Dishwashing Liquids Produce More Suds?

Category: Chemistry

Some types of dishwashing liquids claim to produce extra suds. Do you think it's true? Get samples of several different dishwashing liquids and a see-through jar with a screw-on lid. Fill the jar halfway with water and add a small amount of dishwashing liquid. Then put the lid on the jar and shake for one minute. Measure the height of the foam produced. Repeat with each dishwashing liquid, rinsing the jar well between each trial. Make sure you add the same amount of dishwashing liquid each time. Are some liquids foamier than others?

Chapter 10

Tests Using Toys

54. Air Ball: Does Inflation Increase the Bounce of a Basketball?

Category: Physics

Many objects, including basketballs, must be *inflated* (blown up). Inflation pressure is measured in p.s.i. (pounds per square inch). Does pressure affect bounce? You'll need a basketball and a pump with a pressure gauge to find out. Let air out of the ball until the pressure is 0 p.s.i. Drop the ball from a fixed height, and measure how high it bounces. Then pump the ball to 1 p.s.i. and try it again. Raising the pressure by 1 p.s.i. each time, repeat until you reach the maximum recommended pressure (usually around 8 p.s.i.). What happens to the ball's bounce as the pressure increases? Why does this occur?

55. The Great Escape: Does a Helium- or Carbon-Dioxide-Filled Balloon Deflate Faster?

Category: Chemistry

Just like everything else, gases are made of tiny particles called atoms and molecules. Here's the tricky thing: Gas molecules come in different sizes. Do you think a balloon filled with a smaller gas, such as helium, will deflate faster than one filled with a larger gas, such as the carbon dioxide we push out of our lungs when we exhale? Get two identical balloons. Fill one with helium (most grocery stores can do this for you). Inflate the other using air from your lungs. Then measure the balloons once a day for a couple of weeks. Is there any change in size? If so, which balloon changes more?

56. Super Soarer: Which Flying Disc Goes Farthest?

Category: Physics

All flying discs (Frisbee, Aerobie, etc.) are fun to toss and catch. But do you know which type flies the farthest? Enlist a friend to help you find out. Take several types of discs to your local high school's football field (perfect because it's flat, big, and has measurements printed right on the ground). Stand apart from your friend on the field and start tossing! Move farther apart until you've reached the disc's maximum range. Use the markings on the ground to measure how far each disc travels. What reasons can you find for any differences in performance? (For example, if a flexible disc flies farther than a hard plastic one, find the reason for why that happens.)

57. Pulse Pace: Do Video Games Increase the Heart Rate?

Category: Physiology

Excitement can send a chemical called *adrenaline* flowing through your body. One of adrenaline's effects is an increased heart rate. Is playing a video game exciting enough to quicken your heartbeat? Find out! Measure a volunteer's resting pulse. Let the volunteer play your most exciting video game for five minutes, then measure the pulse again to see whether it has changed. Repeat with as many people as you can. (You shouldn't have any trouble getting volunteers!) What do you find? Why do you think you achieved these results?

58. Bubble Trouble: Which Dishwashing Liquid Makes the Best Bubbles?

Category: Chemistry

Project #53 tested whether some liquid soaps were sudsier than others. Do extra suds translate into better bubbles? Find out! Gather samples of as many different dishwashing liquids as possible. Mix 1 teaspoon (5 ml) of each soap with $\frac{1}{2}$ cup (120 ml) of water. Then grab a friend and a bubble wand and get blowing. You could rate your bubbles by how big they get or how long they last. Which liquid will be the winner?

59. All Pumped Up: Testing the Squirt Range of a Super Soaker

Category: Physics

Super Soakers are the heavyweights of the squirt gun world. Manual pumps on these guns let you put pressure into big water tanks. When you pull the trigger, the pressurized water erupts from the nozzle in a drenching stream. Does the amount of pressure you apply affect the gun's squirting distance? Fill the tank, then pump a few times. Pull the trigger and measure how far the water squirts. Refill the tank and repeat, adding a few more pumps. Keep refilling, pumping a little more, squirting, and measuring until you're happy with your results.

60. Bounce Back: Do Warm Balls Bounce Better than Cold Ones?

Category: Physics

Heat is a form of energy. So warm objects contain more energy than cool ones. Do you think a warm ball will bounce better than a cold ball? What about a hot one? Get four small balls of the same type (for example, tennis, Ping-Pong, Superball). Put one in the freezer, one in the refrigerator, and one in the oven at 100°F (38°C—get an adult's help with the oven). Leave one ball at room temperature. After an hour, gather all the balls (use oven mitts when handling the hot ball). One by one, drop them from the same height. Measure how high each ball bounces. Is there a pattern? HINT: For a prize-winning project, test several types of balls.

61. Go Fly a Kite: The Effect of Tail Length on Flight

Category: Physics

"Plane" kites (those with only one flat surface) need a tail for balance. Tails provide wind resistance and keep the kite from flipping around. Does the length of the tail make any difference to the balance of the kite? To find out, buy or make a simple crossed-sticks kite with a tail. (You can learn how at the library.) Then wait for a windy day. Find an open area and start testing! Launch the kite several times, adjusting the length of the tail each time. Does a long, short, or medium tail work best? Why did you draw this conclusion?

62. Plane Power: Does Extra Winding Equal Extra Distance?

Category: Physics

Rubber bands have a property called *elasticity,* which basically means they are stretchy and springy. Elasticity allows rubber bands to store energy. When you turn the propeller of a rubber–band–powered airplane, you store energy in the rubber band. When you let go, the stored energy turns the propeller, and the plane flies. Will a plane go farther if you wind the propeller more times (in other words, store more energy)? Find out by buying a rubber–band–powered plane. Fly the plane several times at different "powers" (turns of the propeller). Does extra winding (or extra energy) equal extra distance?

63. 3 . . . 2 . . . 1 . . . Liftoff! Which Launch Angle Shoots a Rocket Farthest?

Category: Physics

Most stomp-propelled rockets come with launchers that you can adjust to different angles. Which launch angle will give your rocket the most distance? Your local high school's football field is the perfect place to conduct this test. Set up your launcher on the "0" yard line and adjust it so the rocket points straight up. Shoot the rocket and record where it lands. Then adjust the launcher's angle one notch forward and repeat. Continue until you have tested each setting. Which angle gives you the most distance?

64. A Real Puzzler: Does Jigsaw Skill Increase with Practice?

Category: Psychology

The more you practice most things, the better you get. But what about working jigsaw puzzles? The pieces are in a different order every time you open the box. Do you think practice can help you do these puzzles faster? Get several jigsaw puzzles that are small enough to do in less than half an hour. Time yourself doing each puzzle. Repeat the experiment several times, making sure you take all the pieces apart and mix them up between trials. Do you get faster as you go along? Test a couple of friends if you want to make your results more valid.

65. Downhill Racer: Does Speed Affect Distance Traveled?

Category: Physics

Have you ever coasted down a hill on your bicycle? Once you get to the bottom of the hill, you keep going for some distance without pedaling. Do you think your speed affects your rolling distance? Test this theory with a toy car and a ramp (the back of a cookie sheet makes a good ramp). Set the ramp at a slight angle and let the car roll down it. Measure how far the car travels once it gets to the bottom of the ramp. Little by little, make the angle steeper. (This will increase the speed of the car.) Roll the car and measure its travel distance each time you raise the ramp. Do you see any difference in the car's performance? What can you conclude about the angle of the ramp, the speed of the car, and the distance the car travels?

Chapter 11

Help from Friends & Family

66. Warm Up or Chill Out: Does Warming Up Your Muscles Increase Athletic Performance?

Category: Physiology

As your muscles do work, they give off heat. This is what "warming up" means. The accepted theory is that warm muscles work better than cold ones. Is this true? Enlist several volunteers to help you find out. Pick a physical task, such as running around the block. Have each volunteer perform the task without warming up. Record the times. Wait a few days to allow resting time, then repeat the experiment. But this time, have each volunteer warm up for five minutes first by doing jumping jacks, jogging in place, and stretching. Can they do the task faster?

67. Grab Bag: Can People Identify Objects by Touch?

Category: Perception

Most of us depend on our eyes to help us differentiate between objects all around us. But vision-impaired people rely on other senses, especially touch. Is this ability learned, or does it come naturally? Test to see if your friends can identify objects by touch alone. Get ten bags or boxes and place a different small object in each one. Have several friends feel each object and try to name it. What is each person's success rate? Are complicated objects (such as a TV remote control) harder to identify than simple objects (such as a spoon)?

68. The Nose Knows: Can People Identify Substances by Smell?

Category: Perception

This project is similar to #67. But instead of testing touch, you're going to study smell. Recruit as many volunteers as possible. Get several strong-smelling common substances (cinnamon, garlic, vanilla extract, banana, coffee, tuna, or anything else you like) and put each one in its own cup. Blindfold each volunteer, then ask him or her to sniff each cup and name the smell. Record the answers. Are most people able to identify the smells? Are some smells easier to recognize than others?

69. A Family Feature: Do Family Members Have Similar Fingerprints?

Category: Physiology

No two people have identical fingerprints. But even though no two fingerprints are exactly the same, many are similar. Do you think members of the same family have similar fingerprints? Find out by fingerprinting as many people as possible, including yourself, your friends, and your family. (Look for fingerprinting instructions on the Internet or in books about crime-solving techniques. You can find these books in your local library.) Examine the prints. What similarities and differences do you see? Are your prints more like your friends' or your family's?

70. The Easter Bunny's Nightmare: Are Camouflaged Eggs Harder to Find?

Category: Perception

Some animals can change their skin color to blend into their surroundings. This is called *camouflage*. Does it really work? Find out by holding a paper egg hunt. Cut out paper eggs of many colors. Some should clash with your intended hiding place; others should blend right in. Hide the eggs, then give a young volunteer two minutes to collect as many eggs as possible. When the time is up, record how many eggs of each color were found. Repeat the experiment with a few more volunteers. Are the clashing eggs found more often than the camouflaged ones?

71. Lefties and Righties: The Relationship Between "Handedness" and "Footedness"

Category: Physiology

You know whether you are right-handed or left-handed. But what about right-footed or left-footed? Is there such a thing? And if so, do right-handed people tend to be right-footed? Do left-handed people tend to be left-footed? To find out, get a volunteer to kick a ball. Record which foot does the kicking. Then ask the volunteer whether he or she is right- or left-handed. Record the information. Repeat with as many volunteers as possible. What trends do you notice? Did any of your volunteers say they were ambidextrous (use both hands to perform tasks)? If so, what foot did these volunteers use?

72. Hands Up!: How Does Age Affect the Skin's Appearance?

Category: Physiology

Did you know that skin is a living organ? It's true. And as you get older, your skin gets older, too. It gets thinner, bruises more easily, and takes longer to heal. Do you think older people's skin looks a lot different than yours? Ask friends and family members of different ages to help you find out (parents, grandparents, and older or younger siblings are perfect). Use a magnifying glass to examine each person's hands, from youngest to oldest. What do you notice about the skin? Do some volunteers have smoother skin than others? Whose skin has the most wrinkles? Did the older volunteers' skin look different than your younger volunteers'? If so, how? HINT: Take a photograph of each person's hands for your display. Write your observations about each volunteer's skin under the appropriate photo.

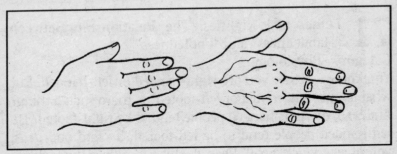

73. Seeing Mind to Mind: Does Telepathy Exist?

Category: Psychology

The ability to read other people's minds is called *telepathy*. Most scientists don't believe it exists. But wouldn't it be cool if it did? Check it out by making your own deck of Zener cards. A deck contains 25 cards (five each of the patterns shown below). Choose one card from the deck and look at it. Without showing the symbol to anyone else, ask a volunteer to name the symbol. Record whether the answer is right or wrong. Continue until the deck is finished. Repeat with as many people as possible. Do your results lead you to believe in telepathy? HINT: Just guessing will yield about five correct answers per deck.

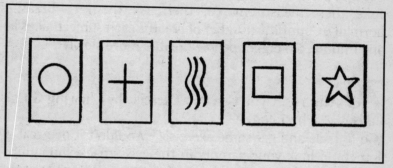

74. Double Vision: Catching a Ball Using One vs. Two Eyes

Category: Perception

Humans have binocular vision. This means that our eyes are separated, with the result that each eye sees the same object from a different angle. Your brain uses this information to decide whether things are nearby or far away. Will closing one eye make it harder to judge distance? Find out with a quick game of catch. Get a soft ball and a friend. Stand apart and toss the ball back and forth twenty times, keeping both eyes open. Record how many times you drop the ball. Now close one eye and repeat. Is there any change in your catch rate? Switch eyes and see if the task is more difficult. If the experiment seems too easy, stand farther apart.

75. Take a Breather: Do Bigger People Take Fewer Breaths?

Category: Physiology

Bigger people have bigger lungs, which means they can take bigger breaths. Do you think a bigger person needs to take fewer breaths than a smaller person? First, decide what you mean by "size." Is it height, or weight, or a combination? Second, test as many people as you can in each category. Take their measurements, then ask them to breathe normally. Count the number of breaths each subject takes in one minute. Do bigger people breathe more slowly?

76. Gum vs. Gym: Can You Exercise by Chewing Gum?

Category: Physiology

"Go outside and get some exercise!" Wouldn't it be great if you could look your parents in the eye, smack your gum, and tell them that's exactly what you were doing? Do this project to see if chewing gum is exercise. Enlist a friend. Measure your friend's pulse rate, then give him or her a piece of gum. Instruct your friend to chew vigorously for five minutes while sitting quietly. When the time is up, measure the pulse rate again. Has it gone up? If so, why do you think that happened? Test as many people as possible. If pulse rates go up every time, you might be able to make a case for gum-chewing as a workout!

77. Chow Down: Do Predictions Match Performance?

Category: Psychology

Does more information lead to better guesses? Find out with a bunch of crackers and two groups of volunteers. Each volunteer will guess how many crackers he or she can eat in one minute, then do a one-minute eating trial. But one group gets no information before guessing. The other group gets to eat a cracker first, just to see what it's like. Does the group that eats the cracker first guess more accurately? HINT: It's OK to test several volunteers at once, but don't let them hear each other's guesses.

78. Stop Staring!: Can You Detect Someone Staring at You?

Category: Psychology

Imagine you're minding your own business when suddenly your skin starts to crawl. You're positive someone is looking at you. You turn around, and sure enough, you catch someone staring! But can you really "feel" the stare, or is it just a coincidence? Test it out. Ask a friend to sit with his or her back toward you. Stare or look away, and ask the friend which one you're doing. Do this ten times in a row, recording the answer each time. How does your friend do? Repeat with as many volunteers as possible. And remember, your subjects will be right about half the time if they're just guessing.

Chapter 12

Cool Stuff to Make

79. Perfect Pitch: A Water Xylophone

Category: Physics

The more matter sound must travel through, the lower the pitch; the less matter, the higher the pitch. Make a water xylophone to demonstrate this principle. Gather eight identical glass containers (spaghetti sauce jars or drinking glasses are ideal). Pour a different amount of water into each container. Then tap each container with a metal spoon and see what pitch you get. Experiment with the water levels until you are happy with the tones. Learn how to play a few simple songs as the grand finale to a winning project!

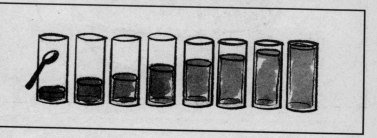

80. Fido's Fantasy: A Self-Filling Water Dish

Category: Physics

To make this ultra-cool contraption you need a large water dish, a jar, and two supports (wooden blocks are perfect). Place the supports in the dish, then fill the dish nearly to the brim with water. Fill the jar all the way to the top. Cover the mouth of the jar, and carefully turn it upside down. Lower it into the dish. Once the mouth is below the water line, remove the covering and set the jar on the supports. As your pet drinks from the dish, the jar adds water to replace what was taken away. HINT: Make sure you explain how this gadget works. Here's a clue: Air pressure. ANOTHER HINT: Supervise your pet every time it drinks from this special dish. The jar could get knocked over. When you're finished recording your data, use the self-filling dish as a cool science fair display!

81. Big Bang: A Model Volcano

Category: Earth Science

You can make a model volcano that spews foamy lava! Build a mound of dirt on a waterproof tray and push a plastic cup into the mound. Fill the cup about halfway with vinegar (any kind will do). Add a few drops of dishwashing liquid and some red food coloring; stir well. In another cup, make a mixture of baking soda and water. Quickly pour the mixture into the volcano and get ready for an explosive result! HINT: Experiment with different measurements to get the best possible eruption. And don't forget to research how and why actual volcanoes erupt. Explain why your demonstration is similar to the real thing.

82. The Plane Truth: Does a Plane's Shape Affect Its Flight?

Category: Physics

Several forces—*lift, thrust, drag,* and *gravity*—are at work when an airplane flies. The shape of the airplane affects how these forces act and therefore how the plane flies. Which shapes work best? Find out by making your own "flying circus." Get a book that shows you how to make many types of paper airplanes. Pick several styles to make and get to work! Before you fly your finished planes, try to guess what they will do. Once you have made your predictions, test them by flying each plane. Did you guess correctly?

83. A Shocking Experiment: Making a Leyden Jar

Category: Physics

A Leyden jar collects and stores static electricity. It can even generate mild shocks on demand! Make one by wrapping aluminum foil around the outside of an empty plastic film canister. Fill the canister about halfway with water, and snap on the lid. Ask an adult to carefully push a nail through the lid, making sure the tip of the nail is in the water. Now rub an inflated balloon against a carpet for ten seconds. Touch the balloon to the nail. Then touch  the nail with your finger to receive a small shock! Don't forget to explain static electricity in your project write-up.

84. Sounds Like Science: A String Telephone

Category: Physics

A string telephone is a cool way to demonstrate that sound travels through solid materials. Get two plastic cups and a piece of string about 20 feet (6 meters) long. Punch a small hole in the bottom of each cup. Put an end of the string through each hole and tie knots to keep the ends from slipping out. Then get a volunteer. You hold one cup; give the other to the volunteer. Stand just far enough apart to pull the string tight. Talk in a normal speaking tone into your cup as the volunteer presses his or her ear to the open end of the cup at the other end. Can he or she hear the words? You can also let the volunteer talk while you listen. How does the sound travel?

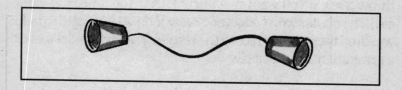

85. Stay Cool: Which Insulator Works Best?

Category: Physics

Sometimes you want to keep hot things hot or cold things cold. To do this, you surround the objects with *insulators* (materials that are poor conductors of heat). You can test the insulating power of different materials by making "melt tanks." Get several identical containers with airtight lids (empty yogurt cups are perfect). Line the inside of each container with a different material. You could try cork, felt, cotton, or anything else you like. Then place an ice cube in each container and seal the lid. Check often and record how long it takes each ice cube to melt. Which insulator works best?

86. Space Rocks: The Effect of Size and Speed on Crater Size

Category: Astronomy

The moon's surface is covered with craters. They were produced when *meteors* (space rocks) smashed into the moon. Do bigger meteors make bigger craters? And does a meteor's speed affect the size of the crater it makes? Find out by filling a cardboard box with wet plaster of Paris (do this experiment outside!). Drop stones of different weights and sizes into the plaster, and measure the craters produced. You can vary the heights from which you drop your meteors. You can even throw a few if you want real force! HINT: You'll need to work fast. The plaster won't stay gooey very long. Ask a friend to help you drop the rocks or record the results. This dry model makes a great science fair display.

87. Invisible Bullets: Building and Firing an Air Cannon

Category: Physics

This cool cannon shoots puffs of air. You'll need a cylindrical container (a cardboard oatmeal tube is a good size). The tube should have one solid end and one open end. Carefully cut a small hole in the solid end. Cover the open end with rubber sheeting (available in hardware stores). Pull the rubber as tight as you can and attach it to the container with sturdy tape. To fire your cannon, hold the container, point the hole at a target, and bang firmly on the rubber sheeting with a spoon. An invisible air "bullet" will shoot out of the hole. You can't see it, but you can prove it's there by making it move a piece of paper or another lightweight object.

88. Fulcrum Fun: How Much Weight Can I Lift?

Category: Physics

Do you think you can lift an adult off the ground? On your own, probably not. But with the help of a simple machine called a *lever,* you can do things you never thought were possible! Get a brick and a thick, long wooden plank. Mark the long edge of the plank at even intervals (for example, mark off every six inches or 15 cm). Then set the plank on the brick at whatever marking you like. Place a weight on one end of the plank and press or stand on the other end to lift. Experiment to see how much weight you can lift at different settings. Do any of the settings let you lift an adult?

89. Twister Tube: How a Tornado Works

Category: Meteorology

Build a model that simulates the whirling funnel of a tornado. Get two empty two-liter soda bottles and remove the wrappers. Fill one bottle nearly to the top with water. Add a few shakes of pepper (this will make your tornado easier to see). Set a metal washer on the mouth of the full bottle, then set the empty bottle upside-down on the washer. Seal the connection with duct tape. To produce a tornado, flip the bottles so the water is on top. Whirl the device a few times. As the water from the top bottle drains downward, a spiraling tornado forms! Compare your twister tube with a real tornado in your write-up.

Sunlight

Colored Light

Fluorescent Light

Incandescent Light

Chapter 13

Appliance Adventures

90. The Right Light: Which Light Is Best for Plant Growth?

Category: Botany

Plants need light to grow. Which type of light is best? You can find out by growing plants under different types of light. First, decide how many light sources you want to test. You could try direct sunlight, colored light, fluorescent light, incandescent light, shade, and even no light. Get one pot for each light you wish to test and plant the same number of seeds in each pot. (HINT: Radish or bean seeds sprout quickly and easily.) Place each pot under a different source of light. Water all the pots regularly and equally. Measure the height of each plant once a week. Do some grow faster than others? Which lights seem best?

91. Singing Seeds: Do Plants Like Different Types of Music?

Category: Botany

Some people like pop music or hip-hop; others prefer jazz, country, or classical. Do your plants care about music? Follow the instructions in #90 to plant and water seeds. But this time, make sure all the plants get the same amount and kind of light. Label your plants with different types of music. For instance, one plant might be "rap"; another might be "country." Every day, put each plant by the radio for half an hour. Let it "listen" to ONLY the type of music on its label. Do some of the plants grow better than others? What conclusions can you draw about your plants' musical tastes?

92. Frozen Flowers: Ice as a Preservative

Category: Chemistry

Objects can be preserved in ice for thousands of years. Test this effect with a few flowers and your freezer. You need five blossoms (the flowering part). Fill four plastic cups with water. Drop a blossom into each cup and put all four cups into the freezer. Do not freeze the fifth blossom; just set it somewhere safe. After a week, remove a blossom from the freezer. Thaw it and make notes on its color, scent, and texture, as well as on the same properties of the unfrozen blossom. Thaw another blossom after two weeks, another after three weeks, and another after four weeks. How do they compare? How does the unfrozen blossom compare with the last frozen blossom that was thawed?

93. The Big Drip: Does Faster-Flowing Water Increase Erosion?

Category: Earth Science

Did you know that wind and water can eat away rock and soil? This is called *erosion*, and the Grand Canyon is an incredible example. It's easy to demonstrate water's eroding power. Just get several bars of soap of the same type and weigh each bar (remove the packaging first). Then leave each bar under a dripping faucet overnight. You can record the rate of the water flow from each faucet in drips per minute. In the morning, remove the soaps and weigh them again. Have the bars you left under faster-dripping faucets eroded more?

94. Hung Out to Dry: Which Technique Dries Clothes the Fastest?

Category: Chemistry

Does a clothes dryer get rid of dampness faster than old-fashioned sunlight? To find out, gather several fabric samples of the same type. (Identical socks or handkerchiefs are perfect.) Get all the samples equally wet, then dry them using different methods. Put one in the dryer; one in the sun; one in the shade; one indoors; one in front of a fan; and others anywhere else you can think of. Check the samples every half hour. How long does it take each one to dry?

95. Plop, Plop, Fizz, Fizz: Does Water Temperature Affect Dissolving Speed?

Category: Chemistry

Alka-Seltzer tablets bubble and fizz in water, dissolving quickly. Do you think the tablets will dissolve faster in water that is hot, cold, or room-temperature? Put one cup of water in the refrigerator overnight. Heat another cup of water (get an adult's help), and leave a third at room temperature. Then drop an Alka-Seltzer tablet into each cup. Time how long it takes each tablet to dissolve. Do they all take the same amount of time? If the times were different, what do you think might account for the difference? Why do you think that?

96. Chill Factor: Do Fans Really Cool You?

Category: Chemistry

A fan doesn't change the air temperature; it just pushes air around. So does it actually cool you? Yes, because moving air makes your sweat evaporate more rapidly, and evaporation causes cooling. Demonstrate this concept by putting equal amounts of water into two identical pans. Point a fan at one of the pans. Place the other pan nearby, but not close enough to get any of the breeze from the fan. Check regularly until the water disappears. (The fanned water should evaporate within a couple of hours; the unfanned water might last a couple of days.) Discuss the reasons for your results.

97. Weather Watchers: Testing the Accuracy of Local Forecasters

Category: Meteorology

You probably have several local TV stations that provide weather reports for your area. Here's the strange thing: The weather forecasters sometimes say completely different things! That's because *meteorology* (the study of weather) involves a lot of guesswork. Are some of your local forecasters more accurate than others? Turn on the TV and watch the news every night for several weeks. Record the weather predictions made by each forecaster. Who is right most often? Which channel do you think is best to watch for weather information?

98. Inside Out: Clothes Reversal in the Washing Machine

Category: Physics

Your parents complain that your clothes are always inside out when they leave the washing machine. But you're convinced that you turned them right side out before putting them into the hamper. Could you both be right? Get an assortment of clothing (try shirts, socks, underpants, shorts, or anything else you like). Make sure each piece of clothing is right side out. Then run the clothes through a washing cycle. Before putting the clothes into the dryer, look at each piece. Did anything turn inside out in the washing machine? If so, mystery solved!

99. Pump Up the Volume: The Effect of Sound Waves on Rice

Category: Physics

Sound travels in waves. If they are strong enough, these waves can move objects. Do you think bigger waves (louder sounds) will create more motion? Find out by pouring a small pile of rice grains on a plate. Place the plate on top of a stereo speaker. Turn the stereo on at a very low volume and record any movement of the rice that occurs. Turn the stereo off and push the rice back into a pile, if necessary. Then turn the stereo on again at a higher volume. What happens this time? Repeat the experiment as often as you like, increasing the volume each time. Does more volume move more rice?

100. Pick-Up Power: Is a Magnet's Strength Affected By Its Temperature?

Category: Physics

When you use a magnet, it's usually at room temperature. Do you think cooling or heating a magnet can change its power? Get four identical magnets. See how many paper clips each magnet can "chain" at room temperature. Then place one magnet in the freezer, one in the refrigerator, and one in an oven (make sure you get an adult's help) at 100°F (38°C). After a couple of hours, take out all the magnets. Be sure to ask an adult helper to remove the magnet that's in the oven. Test each magnet again, including the one you left at room temperature. Do you notice any differences in performance?

101. On a Roll: Do Lighter Objects Require Less Lift?

Category: Physics

Lift is created when the air above an object flows more quickly than the air beneath it. You can demonstrate lift in a spectacular way using a roll of toilet paper and a hair dryer. Insert a wooden dowel through the toilet paper roll. Let a few squares of paper hang down. Holding the dowel at one end, point the hair dryer so the stream of air goes over the roll. When conditions are right, you can create enough lift to unroll the toilet paper! HINT: A full roll probably will be too heavy. Remove paper little by little and test again each time. Eventually the toilet paper will be light enough to unroll.

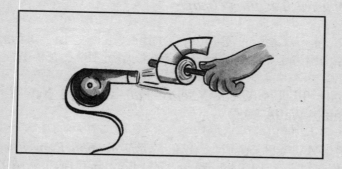

Bibliography

Bonnet, Robert L. *Earth Science: 49 Science Fair Projects.* Blue Ridge Summit, PA: TAB Books, 1990.

Dashefsky, H. Steven. *Microbiology: 49 Science Fair Projects.* New York: TAB Books, 1994.

Frankfort Middle School. *Frankfort Middle School Science Fair.* Accessed September 1999. Internet. Available: *http://www.accs.net/fms/*

The Franklin Institute Science Museum. *Science Activities.* Accessed September 1999. Internet. Available: *http://www.fi.edu/tfi/activity/*

Jones, Gail. "Gender Differences in Science Competitions." *Science Education,* April 1991, 159-67.

Katz, Phyllis. *Great Science Fair Projects.* New York: Franklin Watts, 1992.

The MAD Scientist Network. *Edible/Inedible Experiments Archive.* Accessed September 1999. Internet. Updated 1998. Available: *http://www.madsci.org/experiments/*

Mid-continent Research for Education and Learning. *Whelmers.* Accessed September 1999. Internet. Updated September 26, 1997. Available: *http://www.mcrel.org/whelmers/*

National Center for Education Statistics. *The Condition of Education 1997*. Supplemental Table 22-3, "Percentage of 25- to 29-year-old high school graduates who have completed 4 or more years or college, by race/ethnicity and sex: March 1971-96." Accessed October 1999. Internet. Available: *http://www.nces.ed.gov/pubs/ce/c9722a01.html*

The National Student Research Center. *E-Database of Student Research: Science, Jan. 1993 - Aug. 1999*. Accessed September 1999. Internet. Available: *http://youth.net/nsrc/sci/sci.index.html*

Olson, L. (1985). "The North Dakota science and engineering fair: Its history and a survey of participants." Unpublished manuscript. North Dakota State University, Fargo.

Park Maitland School. *Park Maitland Virtual Science Fair*. Accessed September 1999. Internet. Available: *http://www.parkmaitland.org/sciencefair/index.html*

Science Fairs Homepage. *Primary/Elementary/Intermediate Projects*. Accessed September 1999. Internet. Available: *http://www.stemnet.nf.ca/~jbarron/scifair.html*

ScienzFair Projects. Accessed September 1999. Internet. Updated March 8, 1999. Available: *http://members.aol.com/ScienzFair/ideas.htm*

Science Hobbyist. *Science Fair Idea Exchange.* Accessed September 1999. Internet. Available: *http://www.halcyon.com/sciclub/cgi-pvt/scifair/guestbook.html*

Tocci, Salvatore. *How to Do a Science Fair Project.* New York: Franklin Watts, 1986.

Vecchione, Glen. *100 Amazing Make-It-Yourself Science Fair Projects.* New York: Sterling Publishing Company, 1994.

Vecchione, Glen. *100 First-Prize Make-It-Yourself Science Fair Projects.* New York: Sterling Publishing Company, 1998.

Index